READY, SET, GROW: ANIMALS

A CHICKEN GROWS

by Rex Ruby

Consultant: Beth Gambro,
Reading Specialist, Yorkville, Illinois

Minneapolis, Minnesota

Teaching Tips

Before Reading
- Look at the cover of the book. Discuss the picture and the title.
- Ask readers to brainstorm a list of what they already know about chickens. What can they expect to see in the book?
- Go on a picture walk, looking through the pictures to discuss vocabulary and make predictions about the text.

During Reading
- Read for purpose. Encourage readers to think about how a chicken grows as they are reading.
- Ask readers to look for the details of the book. What are the different stages of the growing process?
- If readers encounter an unknown word, ask them to look at the sounds in the word. Then, ask them to look at the rest of the page. Are there any clues to help them understand?

After Reading
- Encourage readers to pick a buddy and reread the book together.
- Ask readers to name two things that happen as a chicken grows. Find the pages that tell about these things.
- Ask readers to write or draw something they learned about chickens.

Credits

Cover and title page, © Chris Dunham/Shutterstock; 3, © Barillo_Images/Adobe Stock; 5, © erwin_bosman/Adobe Stock; 7, © WDnet Studio/Adobe Stock; 9, © lessysebastian/Adobe Stock; 10–11, © Alter–ego/Shutterstock; 13, © ninell/Adobe Stock and © E.R. Degginger/Science Source and © Jerome Wexler/Science Source and © Eivaisla/Shutterstock; 15, © brozova/Adobe Stock and © saied shahin kiya/Shutterstock; 16–17, © Anneke /Adobe Stock; 19, © Liudmila Chernetska/iStock; 21, © yod67/Adobe Stock; 22TR, © Petr Smagin/Adobe Stock; 22ML, © Nitr/Adobe Stock; 22BR, © Shannon Fagan/Adobe Stock; 23TL, © Judith Dzierzawa/Adobe Stock; 23TM, © Erwin Bosman/iStock; 23TR, © Hamajones/Adobe Stock; 23BL, © Mihai/Adobe Stock; 23BR, © ImagesMy/Adobe Stock

See BearportPublishing.com for our statement on Generative AI Usage.

Library of Congress Cataloging-in-Publication Data is available at www.loc.gov or upon request from the publisher.

ISBN: 979-8-89232-993-4 (hardcover)
ISBN: 979-8-89577-424-3 (paperback)
ISBN: 979-8-89577-110-5 (ebook)

Copyright © 2026 Bearport Publishing Company. All rights reserved. No part of this publication may be reproduced in whole or in part, stored in any retrieval system, or transmitted in any form or by any means, electronic, mechanical, photocopying, recording, or otherwise, without written permission from the publisher. Bearport Publishing is a division of FlutterBee Education Group.

For more information, write to Bearport Publishing, 3500 American Blvd W, Suite 150, Bloomington, MN 55431.

Contents

Wings and a Beak 4

Chicken Facts 22

Glossary 23

Index 24

Read More 24

Learn More Online 24

About the Author 24

Wings and a Beak

A chicken flaps its small wings.

The bird has a pointy **beak** and a large body.

How did it get this way?

A chicken starts life as an **embryo** inside an egg.

It forms when a hen and a rooster **mate**.

The egg grows in the hen's body.

Say embryo like EM-bree-*oh*

In the center of the egg is a **yolk**.

This is wrapped in a watery egg white.

Both are covered by a shell.

The hen pushes the egg out of her body.

She sits on it to keep it warm.

Inside the egg, the embryo starts to grow.

The embryo eats the yolk and gets bigger.

After a week, it begins to form eyes.

By two weeks, it looks like a small bird.

After three weeks, the bird is ready to **hatch**!

Peck, peck!

The chick uses its beak to crack the shell.

The chick breaks free after hours of pecking!

It is tired and wet.

Its body is covered with small feathers called down.

Soon, the chick's feathers dry.

The baby bird gets up.

It follows its mother to look for something to eat.

The young chicken gets bigger.

After about six weeks, it grows new feathers.

The chicken is fully grown when it is six months old.

21

Chicken Facts

Chicks chirp inside their eggs before they even hatch.

A hen can lay up to 300 eggs a year.

The heaviest chicken egg ever was about as heavy as a football.

Glossary

beak the hard, pointy part of a bird's mouth

embryo an animal in the first stage of growth

hatch to break out of an egg

mate to come together to have young

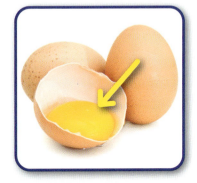

yolk the yellow part of an egg that feeds a growing embryo

Index

beak 4, 14
egg 6, 8, 10, 22
embryo 6, 10, 12
feathers 16, 18, 20
hen 6, 10, 22
wings 4
yolk 8–9, 12

Read More

Anderhagen, Anna. *Chicks: A First Look (Read About Baby Animals).* Minneapolis: Lerner Publications, 2025.

Rice, Jamie. *A Chicken's Life Cycle (Life Cycles).* Minneapolis: Jump! Inc., 2023.

Learn More Online

1. Go to **FactSurfer.com** or scan the QR code below.
2. Enter "**Chickens Grow**" into the search box.
3. Click on the cover of this book to see a list of websites.

About the Author

Rex Ruby lives in Minnesota with his family. He has always wanted chickens. But his family does not want to take care of them.